FOR
Teachers Only

Practical Secrets of Success
for Any Schoolteacher

Vicki Hathaway

with George Hathaway

MJF BOOKS
New York

Published by MJF Books
Fine Communications
322 Eighth Avenue
New York, NY 10001

For Teachers Only
LC Control Number: 2010939741
ISBN-13: 978-1-60671-045-6
ISBN-10: 1-60671-045-1

Printed in the United States of America.

DESIGNED BY LISA CHOVNICK

MJF Books and the MJF colophon are trademarks
of Fine Creative Media, Inc.

QF   10   9   8   7   6   5   4   3

Contents

FOR BETSY, NATE,
AND SARAH, WHO HAVE
TAUGHT ME SO MUCH,

AND

FOR MY MOTHER,
THE BEST TEACHER
I'VE EVER HAD.

Acknowledgments

I'D LIKE TO express my sincere thanks to Scott Messina, Amy K. Hughes, and Lizz Brady at MJF Books for their belief in me and especially for their hard work that has helped make this a better book.

I also want to thank my peers and pals who have reviewed, encouraged, revised, and enhanced this work. Your time, energy, and contributions have been enormously valuable, and I thank you from the bottom of my heart.

Paige Arseneault, Third-grade Teacher

Helen Bentley, Elementary School Parent

Lynne Centore, High School Teacher

Jill Cunningham, School Staff Member

Stacy Giannini, Third-grade Teacher

Katy Hathaway, Fifth-grade Teacher

Susan Mees, Pal

Phil Morton, School Principal and Superintendent

Elizabeth Patria, Language-arts Consultant

In a completely rational society,
the best of us would be teachers
and the rest of us would have to
settle for something less.

– *Lee Iacocca*

Introduction

Welcome to *For Teachers Only*. This is a book by, for, and about teachers. It acknowledges the joys, the frustrations, the rewards, the pressures, the satisfaction, and the value that are all a part of the teaching profession. It's not a university textbook full of teaching theory. It doesn't contain reams of study citations and rambling examples. Instead, this book is a concise collection of more than 130 practical behaviors, perspectives, and specific tips that every educator can begin applying *immediately*.

Teaching fills a very important need in our society. As an educator, you're going to plant seeds of thought and ability in the minds of young people, which will sprout and continue to grow throughout their lives. Their new knowledge and talents will have a ripple effect—a secondary impact on others with whom they connect. As Henry Adams said, "A teacher affects eternity; he can never tell where his influence stops."

The important theme throughout this book is simple: Being a good teacher requires more than just a teaching degree. Success as a teacher ultimately depends on your behavior, both in and out of the classroom. Yes, you must know and apply the best teaching strategies, tools, and techniques that you learned while getting your degree. But you must also be aware of your image, your attitude, and the impression you give your students, their parents, other teachers, your principal, the school board, and the public at large.

The teaching behaviors presented here offer direct, succinct, and practical advice compiled by a professional in the field with more than thirty years of teaching experience. You'll find that they're not very complex. In most cases they need little or no explanation at all. You can read them one night and implement them the next day.

The recommendations have been organized into five chapters:

- Pupils
- Parents and the Public
- Peers and Pals
- Principals and Policymakers
- Principles and Practices

Each chapter contains a brief introduction that establishes the context for the recommended behaviors that follow. The recommendations are presented one to a page and are accompanied by an appropriate quotation from a respected observer.

In the short run, it's easy to *become* a teacher. But to be a really good and effective teacher takes significant hard work and an enormous amount of behavioral change. So, if you're up to it, let's get started. How about beginning with your most important audience, your pupils?

FOR
Teachers Only

Pupils

YOUR NUMBER-ONE *priority as a teacher is your students. Invest the time to understand them and learn how they think and behave. If you do this, and adjust your behavior in accordance with their age and abilities, you will make a big difference in the quality of their learning. Good teachers also understand that they need to treat their students with respect and provide a supportive structure for them.*

This chapter will help you learn to handle a difficult child, reward good behavior appropriately, and motivate your students to succeed.

Establish Your Authority

EVERY TEACHER HAS an important opportunity to establish respect during his or her first time in front of a new class. On day one, introduce yourself as "Ms. Jones" or "Mrs. Smith" or "Mr. Brown"—never use your first name. You are not looking to create a friendship with your students. You're establishing your role as a figure to whom they must show respect. A classroom can be a successful place for learning only if students maintain respect for their teacher's authority.

I was always taught to respect my
elders and I've now reached the age when
I don't have anybody left to respect.

– *George Burns*

Learn Your Students' Names

AS TEACHERS WE should treat our students as the unique individuals they are. One way to signal your interest early on is to learn their names quickly and correctly. Make this a high priority the first week of school. Get the correct spellings and pronunciations down, writing names out phonetically if needed. Match the names to their faces as soon as possible. Create a seating chart that you can use as a "cheat sheet" until you are comfortable with everyone's names. Better yet, play a "stump the teacher" game and incorporate it into your curriculum. Playing with the students, recall as many names as you can each day, tallying and graphing the results and determining your percentage of correct answers. The students will love it, and you will get the practice you need to learn each name.

**The beginning of wisdom is to call
things by their right names.**

– Chinese Proverb

___

Get to Know Your Students

EVERY STUDENT IS unique from every other, and each has a wonderful story to tell. Build a special rapport with each student by learning what makes him or her different. What are her interests? Does she have brothers or sisters? What are the names of her pets? What sports does she like to play? Find out what motivates every one. Keep good notes on each student so you can use what you've learned in classroom situations and in meetings with parents. When you show your students that you see them as individuals, you will demonstrate your respect for them and strengthen your leadership role in the classroom.

As a teacher, I've been learning—
You'll forgive me if I boast—
And, I've now become an expert,
On the subject I like most.
Getting to know you.

– *Oscar Hammerstein*

Start Small

IF YOU'RE A first-year teacher or new to your school or grade level, don't make the mistake of trying to do too much your first year. Stick with the core curriculum. Master the basics. Maintain your vision of inspiring your students with grand ideas and new approaches to the learning process, but stick to your knitting at first and make sure you cover the fundamentals. After some success and more experience, you can begin to test more advanced ideas. But not yet. . . . Be a really good teacher first—the opportunity for greatness will come in time.

The secret of greatness is simple: do better work than any other man in your field—and keep on doing it.

– *Wilfred A. Peterson*

Welcome New Students

HAVE YOU EVER shown up for your first day on the job and found that no one has spent any time preparing for your arrival? Don't let new students in your class feel let down that way. Make a special announcement to the rest of the class in anticipation of the newcomer's arrival. Ask the others in the class to find time at break to say hello. Set up his desk and prepare a "new student checklist" for him. Then assign the new student to a buddy who'll show him around. Small steps like these will go far to help make your new student feel welcome.

**Small cheer and great welcome
makes a merry feast.**

– *William Shakespeare*

Package Your Message

IF YOU WANT to really inspire your students, find ways to "package your message." Incorporate the curriculum in interesting and engaging ways, and learning becomes more fun and relevant. When you teach history, put on an entertaining skit about an event, with members of the class portraying historical figures. For instance, reenact the signing of the Declaration of Independence, the landing at Plymouth Rock, or Rosa Parks's stand for civil rights. Ask each student actor to research and prepare a short script that conveys why the event was historic. Make students active math learners by playing "store" with kindergarteners or simulating Wall Street stock trades in high school classes.

You can have brilliant ideas, but if you can't get them across, your ideas won't get you anywhere.

– Lee Iacocca

Use the News

FROM TIME TO time, when you read or hear something in the news that relates well to your curriculum, consider adding it to your lessons. A news item about water conservation might be included in a science unit. A story about a lost dog found hundreds of miles from home can be used to reinforce geography lessons or turned into a math problem. Use a published interview with your town's new mayor to discuss fact versus opinion in an English lesson. A word of caution, though: Time is precious in today's classroom, so you must learn the difference between teachable moments and interruptions in learning that hold little or no value.

I want all my senses engaged.
Let me absorb the world's variety
and uniqueness.

– *Maya Angelou*

Teach Your Students to Problem-solve

GREAT TEACHERS TEACH children the skills they need to find answers to questions they've never encountered before. This is the ability to problem-solve rather than merely memorize. If children learn skills only in isolation, it will be difficult for them to generalize and apply them in new situations. Instead of just feeding your students information, present it in a larger context. Show students how math skills are used in daily life while you introduce and teach them. Use literature or the students' own writing to present reading or language skills, and include these strategies in their daily practice. Teaching skills in context increases the value of the information and stimulates thinking.

Too often we give our children answers to remember rather than problems to solve.

– Roger Lewin

Catch 'Em Bein' Good

KIDS NEED REGULAR praise from their teachers. Praise can be delivered in different ways, both public and private, depending on the student and the circumstances. You can give a simple, private compliment, such as "Good job, Billy" or "Nancy, I really like the report you wrote." You can hang a public display of completed artwork that includes each student's name. What's important is that you take the time to let students know that you recognize their accomplishments. It may seem a minor gesture to you, but your praise can mean a great deal to the student and motivate her to do more good work in the future.

**Praise youth
and it will prosper.**

– *Irish Proverb*

. . . But Don't Give False Praise

ALL TEACHERS WANT to make a good early impression on their students. Some teachers believe that kids will like them more if they heap lots of praise on them. But kids are pretty smart. They see right through adults who seek their favor by exaggerating their deeds. When your students perform a task well or achieve a milestone, show your appreciation with a measured response equal to the accomplishment. The kids will understand that praise is something special, to be earned, and they'll respect you more for it.

**Praise, like gold and diamonds,
owes its value only to its scarcity.**

– Samuel Johnson

Hold Their Attention

THE BEST TEACHERS know that gaining and maintaining their students' interest in the topic of the moment is vital. Students must be engaged in order to absorb the knowledge they need. Introduce the element of surprise into your teaching: Be animated, make faces, caricature voices, use your hands for emphasis, move about the classroom, wear a costume—even teach from the top of your desk if that will help make your point. If they're watching to see your next move, then you've really got their attention.

**Good teaching is one-fourth preparation
and three-fourths theater.**

– Gail Godwin

Inspire Your Students

CONVINCING A CHILD to do his homework, to study hard for tests, to get to school on time each day—indeed, to do just about anything—is fundamental to the teaching profession. It would be a dream job if all your students were naturally motivated to do whatever is asked of them at school. To inspire a child you will have to go well beyond the curriculum you're teaching. You'll need to employ a composite of soft skills that includes equal doses of desire, commitment, patience, faith, clarity, trial and error, positive reinforcement, and child psychology. The biggest secret to inspiring students is to be inspired yourself—and show it.

The mediocre teacher tells.
The good teacher explains.
The superior teacher demonstrates.
The great teacher inspires.

– *William Arthur Ward*

Instill a Desire to Learn

ENCOUNTERING STUDENTS WHO are turned off to learning or do not value their education is challenging to even the most dedicated teachers. It's your responsibility to find ways to motivate and instill in these students a desire to learn. You'll need to uncover the causes of their negative attitudes and work toward correcting them. Often these students have a history of unpleasant or unsuccessful experiences in school. They may not trust that you have their best interests at heart. Focus on developing a rapport with them by discussing your plan to help them, showing interest in their progress, and letting them know that you're there to help and support them along the way.

**A teacher who is attempting to teach
without inspiring the pupil with a desire to learn
is hammering on cold iron.**

– Horace Mann

Don't Talk So Much

TEACHERS TEND TO spend their entire school day talking. After all, a large part of teaching is conveying information to others. However, the really inspirational teachers know that nurturing a child's learning is maximized when the students fully participate in the process. Encourage meaningful talk by partnering two students for discussion time, and having one report back to the group their combined ideas. Inspire discussion by crafting open-ended questions that require answers with supporting details. When you find ways to get students to talk more than you do, they begin to take ownership of the conversation and learn to listen and accept others' opinions and ideas respectfully.

**Constantly talking
isn't necessarily communicating.**

– Charlie Kaufman

Know When to Back Off

GOOD TEACHERS KNOW their students' limits. Before you assign more class work or a new project, ask yourself these questions: "Am I demanding too much of these kids?" "Could they do a better job if I gave them more time?" "Is this a worthwhile endeavor?" "Could their time be better spent?" The answers to these questions will tell you whether you should dial it back a bit. Remember, you want to challenge, not overload them. When you consider the purpose of the assignments and your students' abilities and limits, you'll be far more successful at helping them achieve the highest quality results.

Some kids want to know why the teacher gets paid when it's the kids who do all the work.

– *Milton Berle*

Keep Everything in Perspective

WE TEACHERS WORK very hard to do our jobs well. In order to be successful, we often feel the need to do it all, do it now, and do it perfectly. This can actually undermine our efforts and have just the opposite effect. As we prepare our students for high-stakes tests, keep up with all the paperwork and documentation our jobs require, and meet the needs of all of our students, our behavior can become very "intense." Remember, your first priority is the education of your students, and they need your calming presence. So when you start to feel the intensity creeping in, take a deep breath, loosen up, and chill out a bit.

If you haven't time to respond to a tug at your pants leg, your schedule is too crowded.

– Robert Brault

Follow a Homework Policy

MOST SCHOOL SYSTEMS have adopted a homework policy that clearly defines the amount of and time allotment for nightly homework. Be sure you know this policy and follow it in your classroom. Make parents aware of it early in the year in writing and again at the fall open house. Set guidelines in your class regarding late, incomplete, and unreturned homework. Will you accept late homework? What effect will late or incomplete homework have on a student's overall grade for the class? Let students and parents know how much time a student will be given to complete work missed because of illness. You will save much effort throughout the year if you implement and convey these policies up front.

**A genius is just a talented person
who does his homework.**

– *Thomas A. Edison*

Make Homework Relevant

WHEN YOU ASSIGN homework, consider the nature of the task and how it can enhance your teaching. Homework is typically practice on a topic you have already taught. Do not frustrate students, or their parents, by assigning problems or subjects that students have not been introduced to or are just beginning to learn. Be conscious of the level of support at home, and do not assign projects that need a great deal of parent involvement. Be creative and assign an engaging and relevant variety of homework activities— this will keep the homework fresh and interesting to the students.

I like a teacher who gives you something to take home to think about besides homework.

– Edith Ann (Lily Tomlin)

Return Homework Promptly

JUST AS YOU expect your students to complete their homework in a timely fashion, make sure you grade and return homework promptly. If you do not, you send a message that these efforts at home lack value and importance. To avoid disagreements about completed and returned homework with either students or parents, maintain a homework log recording the status of each night's assignments for each student.

**You may delay,
but time will not.**

– Benjamin Franklin

Set a Grading Policy

AT THE BEGINNING of the school year, make sure you explain your grading policy thoroughly to your students and distribute the policy in writing so they can bring it home to their parents. Make distinctions between homework, quiz, test, and project grading systems, providing a rubric if possible. Before tests and projects, clearly state your expectations for the work and exactly how it will be evaluated, so the students are clear about what is expected of them. Explain your grading policy at the open house with parents. Your objective, well-explained policies will make it easy for you if you have to discuss grades with parents.

The difference between school and life?
In school, you're taught a lesson and then given a test.
In life, you're given a test that teaches you a lesson.

– Tom Bodett

Explain Grades to Students

WHEN YOU RETURN tests and projects after grading them, be sure to address the strengths and weaknesses of each student's work in your comments. When necessary, speak privately with struggling students, explaining ways that they can improve future grades in your class, using your grading rubric as an example. Maintain confidentiality about your students' grades, in the classroom and out, and never make scores public.

The dream begins with a teacher who believes in you, who tugs and pushes and leads you to the next plateau, sometimes poking you with a sharp stick called "truth."

– Dan Rather

Measure Performance Regularly

CAN YOU IMAGINE what the world would be like if every now and then someone told you honestly and fairly what they thought of the job you were doing and what you could do to improve? Do this for your students and help them succeed. Make the time to sit down with each student and review his or her progress every four to six weeks. Do it objectively, without judgment or criticism. Specify concrete areas on which the student can focus, work with the student to create reasonable goals, and provide thoughtful recommendations. Later, be sure to follow through and review each student's progress.

Leadership is lifting a person's vision to higher sights, the raising of a person's performance to a higher standard.

– *Peter Drucker*

Identify and Monitor Struggling Students

IN SPITE OF all our efforts, we will always have students who struggle academically. We teachers use a variety of proven methods and strategies to help these students close the learning gap. It is vitally important, especially in light of No Child Left Behind policies, to quickly identify struggling students, document our efforts to help them, and monitor their progress. Most school systems have incorporated particular guidelines and schedules for systematically assessing and monitoring the progress of students. Follow these procedures as prescribed. Be sure to keep all testing results, interventions used, and their impact on the students' progress on file and available when needed.

**Dare to reach out your hand into the darkness,
to pull another hand into the light.**

– *Norman B. Rice*

Don't Make Promises You Can't Keep

STUDENTS LOOK TO their teachers for sound guidance and direction. It is wise to assume that every one of them will remember what you promised to do for him or her, whether positive or negative, from "We're going to have a pizza party if you all get an A on this week's quiz" to "You won't have recess today if you complain again about your grade." Be careful not to let them down by failing to keep your word. Don't even hint at something you might not be able to deliver, good or bad.

One must have a good memory to be able to keep the promises one makes.

– Friedrich Nietzsche

Make Eye-to-eye Contact

ADULTS CAN SEEM like giants to young children—
which poses a natural degree of intimidation. When you
need to make an important point or convey a clear message
to a younger child, physically move down to her level and
connect with her eye to eye. Sit or squat next to a child or,
if appropriate, make yourself comfortable on the classroom
carpet. If you remember to make eye-to-eye contact with
your young students, you will be much more effective at
getting your important messages across to them.

**A man never stands as tall as
when he kneels to help a child.**

– *Knights of Pythagoras*

Make Listening Noises

WHEN ONE OF your students needs to speak with you, shift your focus fully to what he has to say. Look him straight in the eye while he's talking to you and use what are called "listening noises," such as "Uh huh," "I see," "Really?," "I didn't know that," or "That's interesting." Your student will know that he has your full attention and that you really do care what he has to say.

Listening, not imitation, may be the sincerest form of flattery.

— *Dr. Joyce Brothers*

Handle Shy Students with Care

IT IS NOT uncommon at the beginning of the school year for students to be a bit shy and hesitant. However, students who are extremely shy need to be handled with particular care. You may think if you encourage them to join social situations they will simply overcome any anxiety they may be feeling. This kind of move can be counterproductive, so tread lightly with very introverted students. Meet with the parents to get their insights about the child's behavior. Discuss with them what is reasonable to expect of their child at this time. Work to gain the student's trust and note the small steps of progress they make socially. If a student's behavior worsens or begins to affect the student academically, include the school counselor or psychologist in further discussions.

**The way you overcome shyness is
to become so wrapped up in something
that you forget to be afraid.**

– *Lady Bird Johnson*

Get Out of Their Way

MANY TEACHERS FEEL their role in the classroom is to impart information to the students. We sometimes forget the goal is to make them independent learners. When we provide too much help, support, and direction, we are signaling to them that we believe they are not yet capable of doing the work on their own. Be sure to give your class just the right amount of support needed and be ready to get out of the way. When allowed to operate on their own, students will have more self-confidence and take ownership of their learning.

**Never help a child with a task
at which he feels he can succeed.**

– Maria Montessori

Stop the Bullying

AT THE BEGINNING of the school year, communicate strongly and clearly with all of your students and their parents that bullying is unacceptable behavior and will be quickly dealt with according to the school system's bullying policy. It is your job to be the first to intercept any bullying that may be going on among students in your classroom. Learn the signs and signals that someone is bullying or being bullied. Document every incident and follow the guidelines your school district has toward bullying.

**You send a boy to school
in order to make friends . . .
the right sort.**

– *Virginia Woolf*

Hold Your Tongue

THERE WILL BE times when a student has forgotten directions, rules, or something you've taught her. Be very careful not to react to your student's lack of focus by embarrassing her. Resist the temptation to say or think, "You should already know this" or "Have you forgotten what we covered yesterday in class?" Instead, stay cool, be patient, repeat the information she needs, and move on.

**A handful of patience is worth
more than a bushel of brains.**

– *Dutch Proverb*

Just Breathe

THERE WILL BE times when you lose your patience with a student or the class as a whole. This can happen for any number of reasons. Your students might not understand the concepts being taught, or they may be particularly distracted or inattentive that day. A student might roll his eyes at you. Or you just might be having a bad day. If you feel you're losing your patience, don't overreact to relatively innocent behaviors. Walk a few steps away, count to ten, and take deep breaths until you regain your composure.

**Teachers who inspire
know that teaching is like cultivating a garden,
and those who would have nothing to do with thorns
must never attempt to gather flowers.**

– *Anonymous*

Maintain Control

MAKE SURE YOUR students know and understand your school and classroom disciplinary policies and regulations, and the consequences of poor behavior. There may be times when a student resists something you need her to do, or openly defies you in a highly disrespectful way. She may even try to bait you into a heated argument. Whatever happens, maintain your composure. Never make derogatory or personal comments to the student—regardless of her age, you could do irreparable damage to her. Have a specific plan for such situations and consistently follow through with disciplinary action. When teachers and students have mutual respect for one another, you've created an environment for academic success. If you're having difficulty controlling your entire class, it's probably time to reevaluate and modify your disciplinary and management techniques.

The secret of education lies in respecting the pupil.

– Ralph Waldo Emerson

... But Make the Punishment Fit the Crime

ON ANY SCHOOL day, you may have several discipline-related issues to handle. An effective teacher knows that all discipline issues are not of equal seriousness. Post your behavior policies and expectations in the classroom for all to see, including the consequences for inappropriate behavior. Be sure the punishment fits the crime, and do not escalate small incidents into major ones. Make use of detention, sending students to the principal's office, or calling parents only when it is warranted. It should be very clear to both students and parents when these measures will be taken.

**When a teacher calls a boy by his
entire name, it means trouble.**

– Mark Twain

Hear Both Sides of the Story

WHEN CONFRONTED WITH a problem or dispute between students in your classroom, be sure to get as much information about the issue as you can. There are two sides to every story, so you'll need to ask each child involved to tell you privately what happened, and listen objectively. Only after weighing all the evidence should you make any decisions or take action.

A child seldom needs a good talking to as a good listening to.

– *Robert Brault*

Set Good Boundaries

AVOID CREATING TOO close a relationship with any one of your students or their families. You might discuss some personal matters such as sports or family activities, but always bring the subject back to the classroom. Be professional and treat every student the same way. If one of them invites you over for dinner, thank him for the offer and politely decline.

The only man who is really free is the one who can turn down an invitation to dinner without giving an excuse.

– Jules Renard

Keep It Professional

THERE MAY BE a time when one of your students shows more interest in you than is appropriate. First, don't cut him off by ignoring him. On the other hand, be careful not to spend more time with him than you do with other students. Maintain a professional student-teacher relationship with him. Don't give him any opportunity to connect with you outside the classroom, be it via your home or cell phone, personal email, home address, Facebook, or Twitter, or any other channel. If the situation continues or escalates, document each incident, and hold a meeting with the student and a school counselor to clearly explain that his behavior is not acceptable and must stop.

The ultimate measure of a man is not where he stands in moments of comfort and convenience, but where he stands in times of challenge and controversy.

– Martin Luther King, Jr.

Go to the Back of the Line

ALWAYS PLACE YOURSELF at the back of the line when escorting your class in school. From that vantage point you'll be able to observe all of your students and ensure that you don't lose anyone along the way. You'll also get to see any misbehavior, in case a complaint is lodged.

**You can observe a lot
just by watching.**

– *Yogi Berra*

Don't Take Yourself Too Seriously

A TEACHER'S PERSONALITY is mirrored in the students and the atmosphere of the classroom. Let your students see that you're human: You make mistakes, crack jokes, and enjoy life just as they do. Don't take yourself too seriously. Relax. Laugh at yourself from time to time. Your kids will feel your ease and it may rub off on them.

**Take everything you like
seriously, except yourself.**

– *Rudyard Kipling*

Turn Mistakes into Learning Opportunities

WE ALL FAIL on occasion. Acknowledging your own mistakes shows your students that it's okay to err as long as you're willing to admit to it and fix the resulting problems. Be sure to explain to the class how you correct mistakes as soon as you discover them. In doing so, you will give your students the guidance they need to be free to admit their own shortcomings and to take the steps needed to fix them. Additionally, you'll impart a lesson about learning from mistakes and doing better next time.

Results! Why, man, I have gotten lots of results.
I know several thousand things that won't work.

– *Thomas A. Edison*

Be a Model for Your Kids

CHILDREN PLAY "follow the leader" all the time. If you want your students to be prompt, then you must be prompt—always show up on time. If you want them to be neat and organized, then you must be neat and organized—clean up your desk, classroom, and files. Set an example as well for personal values, such as integrity, manners, and respect for others. Your students look up to you, all day long. Be a model for them.

**Each person must live their life
as a model for others.**

– Rosa Parks

Look Sharp

YOUR IMAGE IN school is seen by every student, every day. Physical appearance has a sustained impact on the attention and respect students have for their teachers and, thus, their effectiveness in the classroom. Be neat and dress well. Do what you can to stay healthy and fit. Look sharp and make your students proud to call you their teacher.

**What the teacher is, is more
important than what he teaches.**

– *Karl Menninger*

Focus On the Job

IT CAN BE unsettling for students to see their teacher feeling sad, anxious, or on edge. No matter what you are dealing with in your personal life, or among your peers or superiors, don't bring it into the classroom. Once you close that door, your students deserve and need your full attention.

**Focus 90 percent of your time on solutions
and only 10 percent of your time on problems.**

– *Anthony J. D'Angelo*

Stick to the Plan
. . . but Be Adaptable

AS A TEACHER, you make decisions in the classroom every day, every hour, and maybe even every minute. Do your best to stick with every decision. Students become confused when their teacher changes his mind too often. No matter how hard you try, however, there will be times when you may have to change your mind about something you told or asked of the class. If you have to make a change or modify plans, do so. But be honest and explain the reason behind the change so the students understand.

**Indecision
may or may not be my problem.**

– *Jimmy Buffett*

Stay Optimistic

IN TEACHING, THERE are always ups and downs. Your students may not be as interested in learning as you'd like them to be. Some may have something else on their mind. Others hate school. Some may hate you. A few may be disruptive, and their behavior may cause you great anxiety. Look beyond the moment and remember why you're at the front of the classroom in the first place. Remain optimistic. You may find that it's infectious.

**In times of great stress or adversity,
it's always best to keep busy,
to plow your anger and your energy
into something positive.**

– Lee Iacocca

Instill a Sense of Ownership

TEACHERS NEED TO instill a sense of ownership in their students: It's not just a classroom, it's *their* classroom. Each year after everyone's back in school from the December holidays, organize a cleanup party. Assign teams to take over different sections of the classroom. Appoint captains. Give the teams an hour to clean up their section. Then, evaluate the results and award prizes to those who accomplished the most. Do it again in June before the summer vacation.

**Action springs not from thought,
but from a readiness for responsibility.**

– Dietrich Bonhoeffer

Make Students Responsible

STUDENTS LEARN MOST effectively when they have a sense of responsibility and independence. Give them jobs to do each day in the classroom, making sure you fully explain their responsibilities. Foster in them the same sense of independence and responsibility for their academics. Start small, increasing the responsibility of each student while decreasing the support you provide. Implement the "Ask Three Then Me" rule: When a student needs directions repeated or a question answered, he must ask three students before asking you for help. Be mindful of what each child in your class is capable of doing. In time, all will develop newfound self-confidence and a sense that they can accomplish more on their own, with minimal help from their teacher.

A good teacher has been defined as one who makes himself progressively unnecessary.

– *Thomas J. Carruthers*

Remember Birthdays

IF YOUR SCHOOL allows it, say a classroom-full of "happy birthdays" to every kid in your class on his or her special day. Be absolutely certain that you never miss a date or student. Don't forget summer birthdays, vacation birthdays, and weekend birthdays. Students get a kick out of receiving birthday cards from their teacher. Write a short, personal note inside—you'll make their day. Additionally, if you know a peer's special day, and he's okay with it being recognized in public, be sure to greet him with a sincere "happy birthday."

Today you are you, that is truer than true.
There is no one alive who is you-er than you.

– Dr. Seuss

Parents and the Public

PART OF EVERY *teacher's job is to provide good "customer service." You are a public servant, and your customer base goes beyond your students and their parents to the taxpayers in your community. A good teacher understands and respects the expectations of parents and the public. She keeps communication open and doesn't take things personally or let conflicts escalate into emotional terrain. She always finds opportunities to connect her students to the community.*

This chapter describes specific behaviors that will truly improve your relationships with parents and the public. Here you'll learn about communicating effectively with parents, connecting to the community, and representing your school and your profession as an "ambassador of education" in public settings.

Introduce Yourself

WHEN YOU MEET the parents of a student for the first time, be sure to look them in the eye, extend your hand, and introduce yourself right away. Don't present yourself as you would to their kids—tell them your first and last names. "Pat Smith" is far more welcoming than "Mrs. Smith." It's important to put parents at ease and to establish that you are all on an equal level.

**People feel comfortable around someone
who is comfortable with himself.**

– Clay Aiken

Be Accessible

CREATE RELATIONSHIPS WITH parents that invite their participation in their child's education. When you first meet with them, be sure to tell them that you're accessible. Ask them to contact you during school hours if they have a question or concern about their kid's education. Give them your school phone number and school email address. Open communication could be the start of something big—for their kids.

Often, when I am reading a good book, I stop and thank my teacher. That is, I used to, until she got an unlisted number.

– Anonymous

Encourage Parental Participation

SOMETIMES PARENTS NEED a little nudge to get involved in their child's education. Invite those who have not partici-pated to attend their child's class for an hour or two to get an up-close and personal look at what's going on. When they do show up, make it a special event for both the child and the parents. Include the parents in classroom activities, but be careful what you ask them to do. You might think it's no big deal to read a book to the class, but it could be intimidating to some parents. Give them an opportunity to participate at their own comfort level. The results could be amazing.

At the end of the day, the most overwhelming key to a child's success is the positive involvement of parents.

– Jane D. Hull

...But Keep Friendships Out of the Classroom

DON'T ESTABLISH FRIENDSHIPS with the parents of your students. If a parent appears to be coming on strong (e.g., inviting you out for lunch, over for dinner, or to a family birthday party), beware. Thank them for their offer. Explain that your policy is to keep your friendships separate from your classroom, for the good of all the students.

Be civil to all; sociable to many; familiar with few; friend to one; enemy to none.

– *Benjamin Franklin*

Set a Gift Policy

AT THE BEGINNING of the school year communicate your school and personal gift policy to your students and their parents. Especially during holidays, students or parents may give you a gift to celebrate the event or to show their appreciation for the good job you're doing. At times, you may receive something of apparent high value. If a gift violates the policy, give the parents a call and thank them for their generosity. Then explain to them that you're not able to accept. Otherwise, if a gift adheres to the policy, send the family a personal thank-you card.

**There is generosity in giving,
but gentleness in receiving.**

– *Freya Stark*

Say "Thank You!"

WHEN THE PARENT of one of your students does something for you, your class, or the school, express your appreciation right away. The parent's gesture might be a birthday card, help in the classroom, a personal compliment, or an expression of gratitude. Regardless of the occasion, handwrite a personal comment (keep thank-you cards handy in your desk drawer) and send it to the parent's home. Tell him how much his gesture means to you and that your commitment to his child's education is strong and enduring.

**Every time we remember to say "thank you,"
we experience nothing less than heaven on earth.**

– Sarah Ban Breathnach

Stop and Say "Hello"

KIDS GET EXCITED when they see their teacher out in public. When you run into students and their families, take the time to stop and say "hello." Greet the student by name, introduce yourself to and shake hands with the parents, ask them how they're doing, and make some positive comment about their child in school. Be personable and friendly.

Lead the life that will make you kindly and friendly to everyone about you, and you will be surprised what a happy life you will lead.

– *Charles M. Schwab*

Be the Good Teacher Wherever You Go

WHEN OUT IN public, always be on your best behavior. Don't confront others out of anger or frustration. Don't blow your car horn at other drivers unless absolutely necessary. Don't make gestures. And don't say things to others that you'll regret later. In fact, it's good practice to behave as if everyone you encounter might be the parent of a student.

Speak when you are angry—and you will make the best speech you'll ever regret.

– *Laurence J. Peter*

Be an Ambassador

IN EVERY PUBLIC situation, be a good ambassador for your school. Have your class partner with community groups in food drives or neighborhood cleanups. Visit a local senior center, talk with the members, and invite them to visit your classroom. Set up opportunities for your students to volunteer or perform at the center. Have the kids collect redeemable cans and bottles for charity. Always keep in mind that you're more than a classroom teacher in your community.

**Without a sense of caring,
there can be no sense of community.**

– Anthony J. D'Angelo

Involve the Public

INVOLVE THE PUBLIC in the education process and you will reap many rewards. Invite adults from the community to join in your classroom exercises and see how their tax dollars are being spent. They'll see the kids' excitement and how well they are being taught. Make the public's visits to school a learning process for your students as well. If your visitors are senior citizens, ask them to tell your class about their experiences during wartime or other historic events. Encourage questions from the students and keep good notes. Afterwards, ask the kids what they learned from the visitors and why the day was special to them—and to your visitors.

All truths are easy to understand once they are discovered; the point is to discover them.

– *Galileo Galilei*

Tell the World What You're Doing

IT's HARD TO get people involved in your school if they don't know what's going on there. One way to get the word out is to inform your local newspapers or cable television stations about special events at your school. Submit articles about what your students are doing and invite parents and the public to come to school to observe and applaud. Keeping the world informed goes a long way toward creating that special bond with your local community.

As a general rule the most successful man in life is the man who has the best information.

– Benjamin Disraeli

Reach Out Through the Internet

THE INTERNET PROVIDES teachers with fun, easy-to-use tools and facilities for reaching into the community. A school-endorsed website can provide a platform for online conversations, information sharing, academic articles, links to other education sites, blogs, and photo galleries. Teachers can often set up a classroom webpage on the school's site for their students and parents—usually with password-protected access—with news about what's happening in their classroom, such as an open house, homework assignments, and rules and policies. Public areas of the school's website can enhance the entire community's education experience.

Any sufficiently advanced technology is indistinguishable from magic.

– Arthur C. Clarke

... But Beware the Risks of the Internet

IT'S A GOOD idea to use the Internet as an effective communication channel for students, parents, and the public, but be careful if you create a personal webpage of your own. There are a number of online tools in use today that expose personal information to the world. It's easy to register on these websites, and the tools they provide are clever and fun to use. It's wise to set the highest privacy settings available, as over time you may find that you might not want just anyone to view your personal profile, posted comments, answers to personality tests, open messages, and photos and descriptions of events with friends and family. Always avoid interacting with students on these web pages and be extremely cautious about putting your private information into the public domain.

I have never been hurt by anything I didn't say.

– Calvin Coolidge

Attend PTA or PTO Meetings

ANOTHER EFFECTIVE WAY to reach out to parents and the public is through your local parent-teacher association or organization. Good teachers make the effort to attend PTA/PTO meetings. You are the *T* in PTA and as such are a valuable member of the group. Become involved in the association's activities and events for raising money to improve the school or the students' education. If you have suggestions, such as ways to improve the group's relationship with the school staff, make them known. Answer parents' questions about school-related topics. Make your active participation in your parent-teacher organization an opportunity to give the parents a better understanding of how they can positively contribute to their children's education experience.

**We may have all come on different ships,
but we're in the same boat now.**

– Martin Luther King, Jr.

Get Ready for Open House

ANOTHER OPPORTUNITY TO interact with parents and the public is your school's annual open house. This event, usually held a month or two after the beginning of the school year, is a teacher's chance to meet all the parents of his students and also to establish their trust in and respect for him. Prepare well for your school's open house: Think carefully about the message you want to present and how you're going to get it across. Plan to talk about the goals you have set for the class and how you will guide the kids toward them. Discuss what their learning challenges and accomplishments might be. Display examples of your students' work to convey your goals. Explain how you will grade student performance, your policies and rules about homework, discipline, and so on. Answer parents' questions openly and encourage discussion. Make your open house interactive, informative, and maybe even fun.

Parents are like shuttles on a loom. They join
the threads of the past with the threads of the future
and leave their own bright patterns as they go.

– *Fred Rodgers*

Become a Good Public Speaker

It may seem counterintuitive, but teachers often have a difficult time addressing groups of adults, such as the parents of their students, principals or fellow staff, or board of education members. Remember, the skills and strategies that you use every day with your students can be applied when speaking in public. Make sure you are very well prepared, know your content, respect your audience, and make your talk interesting and relevant to the situation. And most important of all, practice.

The human brain starts working the moment you are born and never stops until you stand up to speak in public.

– George Jessel

Prepare Well for Parent-teacher Meetings

MEETINGS WITH PARENTS require good planning. Never show up for a parent-teacher meeting unprepared or empty-handed. Bring documentation of the child's progress and performance, including copies and other evidence of the student's work. Have a goal or outcome in mind, and let the parents know whether there are decisions to make, actions to take, questions to discuss, or problems to solve. Back up your comments, both positive and negative, with examples. Be very specific and to the point, and don't repeat yourself. After each point, give the parents a chance to respond or ask questions. Do your best to create a comfortable dialogue and make the meeting as productive as possible. Don't forget to encourage parents to participate in their child's education and to thank them for their support.

It usually takes more than three weeks to prepare a good impromptu speech.

– *Mark Twain*

Watch Where You Sit

WHEN PARENTS COME to meet with you, be sensitive to where everyone is positioned. If you sit across from parents at a table or desk, you can seem a bit overpowering or intimidating. Instead, hold the meeting at a round table or a circle of chairs. Use the same type of chair as the parents, so you are all on equal "footing."

When you start treating people like people, they become people.

– *Paul Vitale*

Accentuate the Positive

Start each parent-teacher meeting with good news about the child. Tell the parents about their child's accomplishments, positive attitude, hard work, or team spirit. Then give the parents the opportunity to convey their own perspective on their child's progress. This engages them up front on a positive note and makes the discussion a meaningful dialogue for them and for you. It also gives you a sense of what the parents' expectations are and their general sense of how their child's year is going. A positive tone established at the beginning sets the stage for any difficult conversations regarding the student's progress and performance at school.

I always turn to the sports pages first, which record people's accomplishments. The front page has nothing but man's failures.

– Earl Warren

Write It Down

WHENEVER YOU MEET with parents, whether during an informal after-school meeting, at a report-card conference, or at a more formal planning and placement meeting, keep careful notes. It can be very frustrating for a good teacher if her own words are misquoted or misrepresented to others. Avoid the potential for later confusion by documenting the meeting. Record the date and time of the discussion, the people involved, a summary of what was said and by whom (especially you), decisions and commitments that were made, and any unresolved issues. Before you end the meeting, review these notes with the parents.

He listens well who takes notes.

– *Dante Alighieri*

Don't Be Interrupted

WHILE MEETING WITH a parent, if you're interrupted by a phone call, an announcement from the office, or a knock on your door, don't stop the meeting. Apologize to the parents for the brief interruption and immediately return to your business with them. They will see that you value your time with them and have made them and their child a high priority. It's also a demonstration of your respect for them.

There cannot be greater rudeness than to interrupt another in the current of his discourse.

– *John Locke*

Don't Look at Your Watch

DURING MEETINGS WITH parents, don't check the time on your watch or look up at the clock while they are talking to you. Explain the time constraints to them at the beginning of the meeting. Position yourself so that you can see the classroom clock without obvious moves, or ask the parent, "How are we doing with the time?" Show that you respect their time, and the effort they have made to be there, by giving them your undivided attention during the time allotted.

**Tell me to what you pay attention,
and I will tell you who you are.**

– Jose Ortega y Gasset

Know Your Audience

A GOOD SENSE of humor is important in many situations. But when you are meeting with parents, use your best judgment to determine if the parent is in a more serious state of mind and just might be put off by attempts at levity. Based on the atmosphere and mood of the meeting, choose your comments and actions accordingly. You want the parents to leave the meeting having gained or maintained respect for you as the teacher of their child.

**That is the saving grace of humor.
If you fail, no one is laughing at you.**

– A. Whitney Brown

Be Sensitive to Divorced Parents

ALL PARENTS SHOULD receive information regarding their child's progress both socially and academically in school. Be very sensitive to divorced or separated parents of your students. Make and distribute separate copies of progress and report cards, and send invitations to open houses, notices of conferences, and other information to the homes of both parents. Hold a separate conference with each parent if they request this. Above all, keep conversations with each parent confidential.

**When the sun rises,
it rises for everyone.**

– Cuban Proverb

End Meetings Gracefully

UNLESS ABSOLUTELY NECESSARY, do not end a parent-teacher meeting abruptly. Five to ten minutes before your time is up, thoughtfully begin to summarize the important discussion points or results of the meeting. Then, ask questions such as "Do you have any further questions?" or "Before we end, is there anything else you'd like to add?" If you feel the parents need more time, suggest that another meeting be scheduled.

Thoughtfulness for others, generosity, modesty, and self-respect are the qualities which make a real gentleman or lady.

– *Thomas H. Huxley*

Diffuse Confrontations with Parents

IT IS NOT uncommon for a parent to confront a teacher on behalf of his or her child. This usually occurs when report cards are distributed, but it can happen for just about any reason. Remember rule number one: Stay cool. Don't let the parent's emotions get the better of you. Do your best to speak calmly and try to diffuse the situation. Unless you've made a mistake that needs correcting, hold your ground. If the parent refuses to deal with you rationally, you must gracefully end the conversation. Acknowledge that there is a disagreement, suggest that everyone take some time to think about what has been said, and offer to reconvene at a later date. Be sure to document the conversation and let your principal know of any such confrontations.

A long dispute means both parties are wrong.

– *Voltaire*

Gain Their Trust

NO MATTER HOW hard you try to get all parents invested in their child's education, ultimately you will have to deal with parents who hold a low regard for the educational process. They may not understand the importance of parental involvement, they may hold negative views of education based on their own experiences in school, they may feel uncomfortable around teachers, they may be overwhelmed with personal problems, and some just may not care. Work as hard as you can to partner with these parents, learn the roadblocks to success in each individual case, and gain their trust. You will succeed with some, but not others. Don't use a parent's lack of support as an excuse for not providing the best education you can to their child . . . in fact, these are the kids that need you the most.

**The child supplies the power,
but the parents have to do the steering.**

– *Dr. Benjamin Spock*

Be a Child's Advocate

OUR STUDENTS COME to us from a wide variety of home situations and lifestyles. Those from homes that are in chaos or transition often present a very difficult challenge. These students may not have had enough sleep, may have missed meals, and may even be homeless. They come to school tired, hungry, and unprepared to learn. See what kind of help is available to make the situation better for the student. Are there agencies that can provide needed services? Continue to focus on learning with this student, but be aware that he will need extra support and understanding in the classroom.

Unless someone like you cares a whole awful lot, nothing is going to get better. It's not.

– *Dr. Seuss*

Report Abuse

IF YOU SUSPECT that any student is being abused, it is your responsibility to report this to the proper authorities. Make sure you are familiar with the laws regarding child abuse reporting in your state and never hesitate to take action when you feel it is necessary. When dealing with less clear-cut cases, discuss the problem with your school counselor, psychologist, and/or principal.

We all participate in weaving the social
fabric; we should therefore all participate in
patching the fabric when it develops holes.

– *Anne C. Weisberg*

Handle Complaints with Care

WHEN A PARENT complaints to you about another student or parent, follow these steps: If the problem stems from an issue outside of school, recommend that the parent seek outside help. If the problem is school-related, listen carefully, document what you learn, restate what you're hearing, and ask what action the parent wishes be taken. Explain that you will need to learn both sides of the story and that you cannot guarantee any specific action. Depending on the severity of the problem, you may have to involve your principal. Tell the parent the next steps you'll be taking and that you will follow up with her within a specific time. Then do it.

A problem is a chance for you to do your best.

– *Duke Ellington*

Don't Get Involved in Others' Disputes

WHEN PARENTS COMPLAIN to you about another teacher, be careful. This situation can get sticky very quickly. Your only option is to remove yourself from involvement in the complaint. You should never become a sounding board for disgruntled parents. Explain to them that you're sorry that a problem exists, but that the parents need to take the matter up with the other teacher or address it with the school's administration. Describe the process to them and then exit gracefully.

To do nothing is sometimes a good remedy.

– *Hippocrates*

Peers and Pals

A CRITICAL INGREDIENT of a teacher's success is working effectively as a member of the team of teachers that make up the department, the grade, and the school. Effective teachers build strong teams by forging trust, showing respect, and communicating clearly. Good relationships with your colleagues are essential to your enjoyment of the profession, as well as to your ability to perform well in the classroom.

This chapter includes advice for learning from and sharing ideas with others, communicating effectively, socializing appropriately, and resolving conflicts with school peers and pals.

Value Veteran Teachers

SOMETIMES TEACHERS NEW to the classroom believe that they know the latest and greatest secrets of teaching success. They may see veteran teachers as outdated or unaware of the more effective contemporary strategies. Don't make this mistake. Veterans have learned much more than a college course can teach, and they have much to share with you—it's called experience. Take the time to talk with your school's veteran teachers and find out what really works in the classroom and what does not.

**In youth we learn;
in age we understand.**

– Baroness Marie von Ebner-Eschenbach

. . . But Embrace New Ideas

JUST BECAUSE YOU'VE been teaching for thirty years does not mean you know everything there is about the profession. Teachers just out of college may have been exposed to some new ideas, technology, and strategies that can solve problems you've been wrestling with for a long time. Take the time to learn from the novices what's new in the teaching biz. You might be impressed by their fresh and energized spirit and attitude.

I can't understand why people
are frightened of new ideas. I'm
frightened of the old ones.

– John Cage

Mentor New Teachers

AN EXPERIENCED TEACHER who knows the ropes should be there to coach the new teachers in your school. If you've been at your school awhile, volunteer to be a mentor. You will help improve that new teacher's performance, and you may develop an important friendship for life. If you're new to your school and no mentor has been assigned to you, ask your principal for one or seek out someone's wise council.

**Information's pretty thin stuff
unless mixed with experience.**

– *Clarence Day*

Be a Team Player

DURING GRADE-LEVEL, TEAM, planning, or curriculum meetings, don't hesitate to share your resources and ideas with other teachers. You're all on the same team, and the objective of the team is to provide the best education possible for the kids. Don't try to reinvent the wheel. No one teacher has all the answers, but if you collectively share what you know with others, the quality of the team and the teaching goes way up. Don't be insulted if others don't use your ideas right away. Your method may not be their style. But never give up on sharing with others. Over time your example may catch on.

**Players win games,
teams win championships.**

– *Bill Taylor*

Know When to Ask for Help

NEW TEACHERS OFTEN encounter situations that require them to make a decision, solve a problem, or get an answer to a simple question, such as "Who can I go to to get my computer fixed?" or "How do I request materials from the supply closet?" If you're new to teaching, don't waste time with the small stuff. Call upon your peers and ask for their help and advice. With more complex issues—such as, "Should I retain this particular child?"—analyze the situation and examine your options. If you find that after thirty minutes of analysis you are no closer to making a decision, ask for help from an experienced peer. Don't be shy about it. You'll be a better teacher if you learn from others in order to improve your own skills.

It wasn't until quite late in life
that I discovered how easy it is to say
"I don't know!"

– W. Somerset Maugham

Respect Your Support Staff

TAKE THE TIME to get to know the office and maintenance staff in your school. When you need their help, always ask with respect, acknowledge what they have done for you in the past, and don't be demanding. Put important or specific details of your requests in writing, but be sure to discuss your needs with them in person as well. Keep in mind that there may be dozens of people asking for their help all day long. Include them as critical members of your team—you'll accomplish much more in the long run.

**Respect a man,
he will do the more.**

– *James Howell*

Go Above and Beyond

EVERY NOW AND then, do something that your peers and pals in school don't expect you to do. Pick up litter outside or inside the school. Clear the copier jam. Decorate the teachers' room for a special occasion. Make the coffee. It will make an impression on everyone who sees you doing it, and your example may inspire others to do the same.

**Great effort springs naturally
from great attitude.**

– Pat Riley

Clear Up Miscommunications

WHEN YOU AND a peer have a misunderstanding, it's important to resolve the problem as soon as possible. One technique is to repeat what you think you heard and ask your colleague for clarification or confirmation. Never become emotional because of miscommunication, but calmly set about clearing it up. You'll achieve and maintain good working relations with your peers as a result.

**Good communication is
as stimulating as black coffee
and just as hard to sleep after.**

– Anne Morrow Lindbergh

Take Time to Laugh

THERE MAY BE nothing more refreshing and comforting than a good sense of humor. When interacting with your co-workers during the school day, every now and then inject a comment that will bring a smile to another's face. Tell a brief, funny anecdote. Quote one of your student's funny comments. Laugh at yourself, not at others. And never be afraid to smile. A good sense of humor is also an asset when things get stressful, as they are bound to do from time to time. Levity, used discreetly and in the right place and time, displays both intelligence and self-confidence. It can have a very positive impact on the school environment and the relationship among your peers and pals.

One doesn't have a sense of humor. It has you.

– Larry Gelbart

Don't Engage in Workplace Harassment

AVOID ANY PHYSICAL, written, or verbal contact in the workplace that could be interpreted as sexual, sexist, racist, or otherwise offensive in nature. Obviously, direct, sexual contact is forbidden in the workplace. Don't even joke about it. But, other less overt actions have also been deemed workplace harassment. Some examples include telling an off-color joke to a co-worker, putting your arm around a co-worker, giving a co-worker a peck on the cheek, and using vulgar language in the presence of others. Don't forward questionable emails to others in your school. Err on the side of caution in all such matters—if you sense that something might be taken as harassment, don't do it.

Morality, like art, means drawing a line someplace.

– *Oscar Wilde*

Don't Join Cliques

BE AWARE OF your school's culture and workplace politics. Groups or cliques of staff members can create stress and division among employees in your school. Do your best to resist peer pressure; avoid becoming part of a clique and maintain a professional working relationship with everyone.

You must be the change you wish to see in the world.

– Mahatma Gandhi

Be Sensitive to Others

YOU WILL BECOME good friends with some of your peers in school. Be sensitive to your colleagues with whom you don't socialize. Don't pass around photos or discuss events or activities to which they weren't invited at school. Follow the golden rule and treat others as you would like them to treat you.

Really big people are, above everything else, courteous, considerate, and generous.

– Thomas J. Watson, Sr.

Don't Gossip

NEVER GOSSIP ABOUT or criticize your peers. Chances are that your words will only come back to haunt you. Avoid the temptation to join in condemnation of another teacher or staff member, including your principal. Instead, try to change the subject to something more positive. If the conversation continues, find a reason to leave the discussion.

Any fool can criticize, condemn, and complain—and most fools do.

– Benjamin Franklin

Don't Blame Others

IF YOU'RE A third-grade teacher, you start the year with a second-grade class. In a perfect world, all the students would have passed all the tests and have the required skills and knowledge to be in your classroom. But in the real world, some students may be missing the knowledge they need. When that's the case, take a deep breath, relax, and resist the temptation to say something like, "Didn't Mrs. Smith teach this to you?" Assume Mrs. Smith did teach her class everything they needed to know. Keep your reaction cool and calm. Remember it's your job to take your students from where they are to where they need to be—not to blame your peers for failing to do their job.

I always prefer to believe the best of everybody. It saves so much trouble.

– Rudyard Kipling

Resolve Conflicts in Private

A DISAGREEMENT WITH a fellow teacher should never be aired in public or in front of students. Suggest that you find a quiet, private place to discuss the problem. Even behind closed doors, be sure to maintain a calm, level-headed tone. Explain that you want to resolve your differences quickly and in a win-win fashion. State your side of the issue in concise, clear language, and ask for understanding. Listen to your peer's perspective on the problem, and do your best to see her view. If this does not clear the air, agree that you'll disagree, that you need to revisit it later, or that you need independent mediation. Don't share the problem with others unless you have both agreed to bring in a third party.

Reprove thy friend privately;
commend him publicly.

– *Solon*

Don't Take Disagreements Personally

THERE IS NO room in a school setting for animosity between co-workers. Do your best not to take things personally when you and another don't see eye to eye. This might be a challenge, especially if your peer actually intended for a comment or action to be personal in nature. Assume not—and never cross that line yourself.

**Wisdom is what's left after
we've run out of personal opinions.**

– Cullen Hightower

Offer Counsel When Needed

IF YOU DISCOVER that a fellow teacher is having a problem, it might be appropriate to bring it up with him, depending on the relationship you and he have. Perhaps he's struggling with teaching a particular subject, experiencing some frustration with his students, or is just not as successful in the classroom as he'd like to be. Approach him in a private setting and try something like, "I struggled with second-grade math myself when I first began teaching. Would you be interested in talking about it? You might find my own experiences helpful." Assure your colleague that you will keep your talk confidential, and don't discuss the issue with anyone else.

I always wanted to be somebody. If I made it, it's half because I was game enough to take a lot of punishment along the way and half because there were a lot of people who cared enough to help me.

– *Althea Gibson*

Attend Funerals and Weddings

WHEN A CO-WORKER has a death in the family, show your respect and concern for her by attending the funeral or the wake or sending a sympathy card. If you receive an invitation to the wedding of a fellow teacher's child, be sure to attend or send a nice gift or a congratulatory card. When colleagues face other challenges, send "get well" or "thinking of you" cards. These personal connections among peers can go a long way toward strengthening your trust in and respect for one another during the workday.

**Go to other people's funerals,
or they won't go to yours.**

– Yogi Berra

Socialize with Your Peers

MAKE TIME TO socialize with your peers outside of school. Attend birthday or retirement parties, softball games, happy hours, professional sporting events, dinner parties, tours, and other excursions and gatherings. Opportunities to strengthen relationships with co-workers outside of the classroom lead to greater trust and respect in the workplace. As noted earlier, don't talk about the event in front of teachers who were not invited.

**Life may not be the party we hoped for,
but while we're here we should dance.**

– Anonymous

Send Holiday Greetings

THE END-OF-YEAR HOLIDAY season is a joyous time. You decorate your classroom. You sing holiday songs. You may discuss holiday traditions with the class. It's also a time to send out holiday greetings to your co-workers. Sending all those cards is a lot of work, but the gesture will be rewarded by the good fellowship you instill in others.

Celebrate the happiness that friends are always giving, make every day a holiday and celebrate just living.

– Amanda Bradley

Principals and Policymakers

ONE OF THE *most important lessons a teacher can learn is how to get along with the principal, the superintendent, and the school board. They manage the team and make the policies for your school district. Getting them on your side is essential, for you and your students.*

This chapter includes recommendations for making meetings with your principal more productive, respecting your principal's role and availability at school, and gaining the recognition for the work you and your peers are doing.

Respect Your Principal's Role

IN MANY SCHOOL systems, the principal oversees dozens of professionals, paraprofessionals, and staff members, and thus is unable to deal with everyone's day-to-day concerns and issues. Discuss with your principal the types and severity of issues she wants to be apprised of immediately. Try solving all other issues on your own or with your network. Discuss maintenance problems with the building custodians, student performance with the parents, routine academic issues with your colleagues in their area of expertise, and social issues with school counselors. Avoid discipline issues through solid, consistent class management. Doing your part will free your principal to focus on the most pressing issues in the school.

If you have time to whine and complain about something, then you have the time to do something about it.

– Anthony J. D'Angelo

Make Meetings with Your Principal Productive

BECAUSE YOUR PRINCIPAL is so busy, you'll need to value the times when you're able to meet with her. Prepare well for the meeting, arrive on time, be concise and to the point, and be flexible if the principal is interrupted by some administrative emergency. Begin your meeting by asking if she can still meet with you as planned. Remind her of the topic for your discussion and what outcome you hope to achieve from the meeting. Bring copies of important materials, and prefill any forms that you need her to sign. Throughout the meeting, take good notes, ask for the principal's feedback and opinion, and seek suggested actions you might need to take.

**Before anything else,
preparation is the key to success.**

– *Alexander Graham Bell*

Make Your Case

WHEN YOU HAVE an idea for improving the quality of education, you'll need to convince your principal it has value. Research your idea and list the benefits for the students and the school. State how the action will increase learning. Talk to other schools and teachers who've done it before, and quote them in your documentation. Prepare a solid, clear, informative, computer-generated proposal that includes all of this information in a professional way.

Good ideas are not adopted automatically. They must be driven into practice with courageous patience.

– Admiral Hyman Rickover

Update Your Principal

ONCE YOU'VE GAINED support for your new ideas, it's important to form an ongoing partnership with your principal. Make it a habit to follow up and report to him the progress you've made or the results you've achieved. You and your teammates should schedule a regular status review with him. Remind the principal of the problem you're solving or the ideas you're implementing. Describe or list the steps you and your team have taken. Give clear examples of your results so far. Demonstrate how the whole school—its students and its teachers—has benefited. Ask for agreement that you've made good progress and confirm the next steps.

**Never doubt that a small group of
thoughtful, committed people can change the world.
Indeed, it is the only thing that ever has.**

– *Margaret Mead*

Treat Your Principal as a Colleague

WATCH FOR OPPORTUNITIES to strengthen your partnership with your principal in a collegial way. Touch base briefly in the hallway about a change in the curriculum or a struggling student's improvement. Stop by the principal's office to say "good morning" and mention how well one of your classroom projects is going. Ask him for his feedback on how well you ran the school assembly. Keeping your principal informed and seeking ideas and feedback on a regular basis is good for your principal and for your success as a teacher.

The more elaborate our means of communication, the less we communicate.

– *Joseph Priestley*

Educate Your Principal

EXCITING TEACHING IS going on in your classroom every day. You may have finished a particularly successful interactive science unit or invited the parents to a class activity, or you may be celebrating the recent accomplishments of your students. Invite your principal to be part of these events. It will give her the opportunity and time to become better educated about your students and perhaps their parents, learn more about the curriculum at your grade level, and observe challenging or difficult students that you may have discussed with her. And she will see the innovative strategies and teaching techniques you are incorporating in your class each day.

**Be in charge of your own
destiny or someone else will.**

– Jack Welch

Abide By Your Principal's Contact Policy

EACH PRINCIPAL HAS her own preferred way of communicating with her staff. Whether it is email, voice mail, written notes, or through office assistants, use it as your first channel of contact. Ask when it is appropriate to call her at home or on her cell phone. In addition, follow through with some form of written communication as a record of your contact with the principal. Along the same lines, find out the types of information she wants sent directly to her and what can be handled through her assistants. Understanding and following your principal's contact policy up front may eliminate headaches down the road.

**The new electronic interdependence recreates
the world in the image of a global village.**

– *Marshall McLuhan*

Keep Your Principal Informed

MOST ISSUES RELATING to your students and/or their parents can be addressed and resolved without intervention. At times, however, an ongoing concern about an individual student or parent may require the attention of your principal. Document the situation when it first arises, whether it's an academic or social concern about a particular student or an unresolved matter with a parent regarding her child's education. Use these notes when you report the situation to your principal, and keep her updated regularly in writing about your concerns and the actions you've taken. You'll thus create an invaluable resource and record for her in the event that she becomes directly involved in the resolution of the matter.

To effectively communicate, we must realize that we are all different in the way we perceive the world and use this understanding as a guide to our communication with others.

– Tony Robbins

113

Schedule Additional Evaluations

EVERY SCHOOL DISTRICT has a process in place for evaluating its teachers. It usually includes annual goal-setting and one or two formal observations by your principal followed by meetings to assess, discuss, and reflect on the observations and your overall progress toward your goals. If you are a first-year or new teacher in a district or have had poor reviews in the past, it would be to your advantage to schedule additional formal observation and feedback sessions with your principal. Inviting the principal into your classroom for additional review signals your desire to improve your instruction techniques and your willingness to accept constructive criticism.

The greatest danger for most of us is not that our aim is too high and we miss it, but that it is too low and we reach it.

– *Michelangelo*

Respect Even a Difficult Principal

NO MATTER HOW good a teacher you may be, you just might end up in a school with a difficult principal. Until you have her full confidence, you have close to no chance of changing her mind or making her a more effective leader. Never make your opinions public. Stick to your duties, be the best teacher you can be, and maintain the best working relationship you can. Be respectful of your principal, and you're likely to have respect returned in kind.

Leadership is based on inspiration, not domination; on cooperation, not intimidation.

– *William Arthur Wood*

Stand Up . . .

ACTIONS AND DECISIONS made by principals, superintendents, or school boards may contradict what we know best as teachers. Parents might demand special treatment for their child through your principal. The board might propose budget cuts to programs that are critical to the students' education. When you believe that something is getting in the way of the best education you can provide your students, you must stand up and express your concerns, and what you think should change, to your principal or teachers union. Be respectful and clearly state the issue. If you let the problem go, you might not be able to address it later.

**Our lives begin to end
the day we become silent
about things that matter.**

– *Martin Luther King, Jr.*

... But Know When to Stand Down

YES, YOU CAN disagree with your principal about issues related to your students' education. You might even debate these issues with her. But be aware that if you're particularly adamant about the topic, your passion might be perceived as anger, and your message could get lost if you turn it into an argument. Then no one wins. Instead, state your position, back it up with hard evidence, and do your best to find common ground. In the end, however, the decision lies with your principal.

Knowledge is learning something every day, wisdom is letting go of something every day.

– Zen Proverb

Draw the Line

WHEN YOU FEEL that your principal is delegating too many tasks to you, let her know what you can and cannot do. List in priority sequence the tasks that you have to accomplish each day or week. Then draw a line at the task below which you don't have enough time left to cover. Sit down with your principal and explain that you can complete the tasks above the line but not those below. Suggest that lower-priority tasks be delegated to others or put on the back burner. If they can't, suggest that you might be able to do the tasks in segments over a longer period of time.

**Accomplishing the impossible means only
that the boss will add it to your regular duties.**

– Doug Larson

Presenting to the School Board

YOUR PRINCIPAL MAY ask you to give a presentation to the school board on an educational issue. In such cases, first get input from your principal and/or superintendent about the exact nature and content of the topic. Research and formalize your presentation, and preview it with your principal and/or superintendent. When you are before the board, be professional and be ready to answer any questions they might ask.

The best way to sound like you know what you're talking about is to know what you're talking about.

– *Anonymous*

Don't Compromise Your Vote

DO NOT FEEL that you are required to vote on a bill or proposal as your union requests. You are an independent citizen regardless of your political affiliations, with the right to your own opinions and beliefs. If the union represents your beliefs, then support them in their efforts. If you do not agree, you have every right to exercise your freedom of speech.

**Peace won by the compromise of principles
is a short-lived achievement.**

– Anonymous

Seek Union Help When Needed

THERE WILL BE times throughout your teaching career when you may have problems with your school's administration. You might feel that the principal did not give you a fair performance rating. You might have a dispute with her over your adjunct duties around the school. Whatever the problem, your first course of action must be to present your concerns to your principal. If you feel that you're not getting anywhere with her, you should turn to the teachers union. The union is typically a collective bargaining unit, but is also your advocate for management and administrative issues. You pay union dues each month—so don't hesitate to get your union on your side.

Asking for help does not mean we are weak or incompetent. It usually indicates an advanced level of honesty and intelligence.

– Anne Wilson Schaef

Principles and Practices

FINALLY, TRULY EFFECTIVE *teachers exhibit overarching behaviors, attitudes, leadership skills, and personal attributes that strengthen their value to the profession. In addition to the behaviors and tips already provided, these "Principles and Practices" can be applied in any and all encounters with your students, their parents, the public, your colleagues, and the school administration.*

The recommendations in this chapter will help enhance every aspect of your teaching life and increase your effectiveness as an educator. You'll learn, for example, about demonstrating integrity, showing respect to all, practicing reflection, and becoming a lifelong learner.

Be Passionate

You're a teacher, and you won't be doing your job well if you are not passionate about your profession. Be driven to achieve all that you can as an educator. Speak out if someone or something is distracting you from providing a quality education to your students. Demonstrate your enthusiasm wherever and whenever you can. Invest your extra energy and time in projects that will benefit your school.

My passions were all gathered together
like fingers that made a fist.
Drive is considered aggression today;
I knew it then as purpose.

– *Bette Davis*

Become a Good Salesperson

JUST BECAUSE YOU'RE a teacher doesn't mean that your pupils, their parents, or even your peers will always agree with you. Sometimes you have to work at convincing others to accept your ideas. This takes understanding, wisdom, patience, clarity, and salesmanship. You'll need to shape your message in such a way that you get and hold their attention. State the facts clearly and concisely. Plan ahead for any challenges that might come up and how you're going to respond. Keep in mind that you can succeed at selling to others only things you truly believe in.

**Before you try to convince anyone else,
be sure you are convinced, and if you cannot
convince yourself, drop the subject.**

– *John H. Patterson*

Take Responsibility for Your Message

AN IMPORTANT LEADERSHIP principle is: If others don't understand you, it's not their fault—it's yours. When your message doesn't seem to be getting through to students, parents, peers, the principal, or someone else, try to find another way to communicate it. Be descriptive. Give examples. Try a metaphor or two. Draw analogies. Tell a story that reinforces your point. If they still don't understand, ask them questions. What is their understanding? What doesn't make sense to them? Do they have a different life experience, and thus perspective, that you might need to hear? This takes time and energy, but clarity and understanding are your responsibility, not theirs.

It is not so much the content of what one says as the way in which one says it. However important the thing you say, what's the good of it if not heard or, being heard, not felt.

– Sylvia Ashton-Warner

Ask Good Questions

ATTEND SCHOOL-RELATED MEETINGS—those with your peers, parents, principals, or the teachers union—prepared to ask good questions. If you don't find out all you need to know, the meeting is a waste of your time. Remember that good questions are pertinent to the topic, general enough that everyone learns from the answer, and haven't already been asked in different words. Be a really effective educator and seek good answers to your good questions.

**Judge a man by his questions
rather than his answers.**

– Voltaire

... Then Listen and Learn

IT SOUNDS SIMPLE, but it's sometimes difficult for a good teacher to stop talking and begin listening. When you ask questions of your peers, parents, the principal, or others, be sure to listen carefully to their answers. Take good notes. Seek information you don't have. Ask for clarification of an idea or proposal. Don't presume that you have all the answers. You'll be surprised at what you can learn as a teacher.

**A good listener is not only popular everywhere,
but after a while he gets to know something.**

– *Wilson Mizner*

Keep Up Your Own Training

IN SOME STATES the minimum training required to maintain your teaching certificate may not be enough for the good of your classroom. If you really want to provide the education your students deserve, go beyond the minimum. Attend seminars, professional conferences, or Internet-based webinars on new teaching strategies, classroom computer tools, and the latest research on student motivation or the learning process.

**Who dares to teach
must never cease to learn.**

– *John Cotton Dana*

Learn to Juggle

A FEW OF the activities a teacher typically needs to juggle are lesson plans (priority one), grading homework, classroom discipline, reports, parent calls, bus duty, meetings, conferences, school board actions, principal requests, disagreements with other teachers, filing and organizing, recess, school nurse visits, fights, emergencies, special needs, bullying, computer glitches, copier jams ... the list seems endless. The key to teacher sanity is effective time management. Learn to plan ahead, prioritize tasks, set time limits, delegate to others, and computerize as much as you can. And by all means, don't procrastinate.

A teacher's day is one-half bureaucracy, one-half crisis, one-half monotony, and one-eightieth epiphany. Never mind the arithmetic.

– Susan Ohanian

Use Your Network

KEEP YOUR CONTACT list of former professors, fellow teachers, parents, and other colleagues up to date. When you're facing a problem with a student, a parent, another teacher, or the principal, reach out to someone in your network who might have suggestions on how to handle the situation. You'll be amazed at how easy it will be and how great the reward.

Call it a clan, call it a network,
call it a tribe, call it a family.
Whatever you call it, whoever
you are, you need one.

– *Jane Howard*

Get Organized

IT'S HARD TO be a successful teacher if you are disorganized. Clear your desk. Manage your file folders. Get your paperwork under control by doing one of the following with each sheet of paper in front of you: File it, trash it, send it, delegate it, or shred it. When your workplace is under control, you'll feel more focused on the really important priorities.

Don't agonize.
Organize.

– Florynce R. Kennedy

Put In Extra Hours

THE NUMBER OF responsibilities that a teacher has can be overwhelming. One solution to keeping all those balls in the air is to put in extra hours. Start your day an hour before class begins and spend an extra hour after class ends. Use these two hours to prepare for and follow up on your day's classes. You'll get control of the chaos and, in time, you'll develop a routine that will require fewer extra hours. You'll also need to put in extra hours before school begins in the fall, as you plan for the new school year.

Time flies like an arrow.
Fruit flies like a banana.

– *Groucho Marx*

Stay Fully Focused

IF YOU'RE PLANNING a vacation, worried about a car problem, concerned about your child's dentist appointment, thinking about a trip to a professional conference, or have your mind on any other outside activity, you aren't 100 percent on the job. Until you're outside of school, stay focused on your classroom. Never let outside distractions interfere with your work. When you return to school from some time away (e.g., a holiday, a school vacation, summer off, or a family illness), get right back to school mentally and stay fully focused.

**You can't depend on your eyes
when your imagination is out of focus.**

– *Mark Twain*

Face Problems Head-on

DO NOT AVOID or dismiss problems—they will eventually end up on your doorstep. And don't wait for problems to come to you. Take the initiative in resolving disagreements with colleagues. Don't hesitate to inform parents when their child is struggling in school. Be strong. Don't back off. Instead, anticipate, plan your moves, and face the problem head-on.

What is bad?
All that proceeds from weakness.

– Friedrich Nietzsche

Don't Be Afraid to Take Risks

ALWAYS BE ON the lookout for opportunities to improve, modify, or adjust your approaches to teaching and interactions with others. Take action. Take risks. Be the first to try out new ideas. Evaluate situations and make decisions. Your peers, pupils, parents, and the principal will be impressed with your performance and more confident in you as a "get it done" teacher.

Fortune favors the bold.

– Virgil

Always Be on Time

DEVELOP THE HABIT of being on time for meetings and appointments. Show everyone with whom you meet that he or she is important and show up on schedule. Set up the electronic calendar software on your computer so it sends a reminder or sounds an alarm well in advance of every meeting. Being punctual is a sign of maturity, responsibility, and respect for others.

**The trouble with being punctual
is that nobody's there to appreciate it.**

– Franklin P. Jones

Make Use of Technology

COMPUTER LITERACY IS a given in today's classroom. Go beyond the basics and discover ways to use technology to enhance the learning experience in the classroom. Find out how to make effective PowerPoint slides, and use a projector to present your slides to your class or on parents' night. Make use of network sharing and other configurations your school has set up. Create a page on your school's website to provide your students and their parents with resources, tools, and information that will enhance the students' education experience. Maintain a list of your favorite websites and keep it current on your classroom webpage. Be as passionate about your technology skills as you are about your teaching skills.

**I do not fear computers.
I fear the lack of them.**

– Isaac Asimov

138

Always Tell the Truth

"TELL THE TRUTH" seems so simple an axiom, but we are often surprised to discover that someone we know has not been truthful. Dishonesty tears at our integrity and makes others lose faith in and respect for us. Keep one thought in mind. As a teacher and as a human being, if you don't tell the truth, eventually it will be discovered that you lied. This is especially costly if your students discover you lied to them.

I don't want any yes-men around me.
I want everybody to tell me the truth
even if it costs them their jobs.

– *Samuel Goldwyn*

Demonstrate Integrity

INTEGRITY IS MULTIDIMENSIONAL. Besides honesty and principles, it encompasses reliability, honor, and sincerity. Seek every opportunity to demonstrate your integrity in and out of the classroom. Do your best to engender trust and respect. Do what's ethically right, and try not to let people down. The difference between being a good teacher and becoming a really great one just might be in the level of integrity you demonstrate each day.

Real integrity is doing the right thing, knowing that nobody's going to know whether you did it or not.

– *Oprah Winfrey*

Remember: "I Could Be Wrong"

TEACHERS ARE EXPECTED to have correct answers to just about every question. Your tendency to "be the expert" will be strong, even outside the classroom. But you don't know everything. A very effective way to remember this is to say to yourself, "I could be wrong." Don't press others with your "facts." You might be embarrassed to discover that you are wrong.

Facts are stubborn things. . . .

– *John Adams*

Be Honest About Your Mistakes

NEVER BE AFRAID or reluctant to admit that you were wrong. Apologize to a parent when you forget to make a promised phone call. If you miss a meeting, let the attendees know that you're sorry for muddling your schedule. When you fail to deliver a lesson from your plan book, don't blame anything or anyone else but yourself. A few errors here and there will never trump the many accomplishments you master along the way.

**Nobody stands taller than
those willing to stand corrected.**

– William Safire

Control Your Emotions

RAISING YOUR VOICE, or worse yet, yelling at someone, demonstrates a lack of self-control. Your constituents will lose faith in you as an effective teacher. If you feel yourself losing it, take a deep breath, count to ten, and smile. The truly great teachers have learned to control their emotions. This helps them maintain the respect from others that they need to be really successful.

**The sign of an intelligent people
is their ability to control emotions
by the application of reason.**

– *Marya Mannes*

Watch What You Say

WE TEACHERS HAVE to be extra careful to watch what we say to everyone, whether in the classroom, teachers lounge, office, or out in public. The best approach is to assume that everything you say will be published or broadcast to the world. Ensure that what you do say is appropriate, clear, and precise and cannot be misinterpreted—especially by your students and their parents.

Children seldom misquote.
In fact, they usually repeat word for word
what you shouldn't have said.

– Anonymous

Exercise Your Rights

THERE MAY BE a time when a candidate for an elected office asks for your support. She might ask you to donate to her campaign, work as a volunteer, or place her sign on your lawn. As a teacher—a public figure in your community—should you do it? The answer is simple: You are a citizen and a taxpayer first and foremost. Your right to free speech cannot be abridged. If and when you do support a particular nominee, don't be afraid to be public about it. But never promote the candidate in your workplace. Don't even wear a campaign button to school.

One of the penalties for refusing to participate in politics is that you end up being governed by your inferiors.

– Plato

Be Reflective

THE BEST TEACHERS continue to learn and grow throughout their entire careers. Whether you are teaching a lesson or interacting with a student, parent, principal, or peer, take time to reflect on your performance in light of how it can be improved for the future. Ask: "How can I improve this lesson so that it better meets the needs of the students?" "What can I do to improve communications with parents?" "How can I partner better with the public?" "Why did [or didn't] this work?" Keep a journal and jot down short reflections and reminders, with an eye for improvement. Make time to reflect on your actions and don't be afraid to honestly assess your behavior. You will become a much better teacher for the effort.

The illiterate of the 21st century will not be those who cannot read or write, but those who cannot learn, unlearn, and relearn.

– Alvin Toffler

Respect Everyone

THERE ARE GOING to be times when you have to deal with people who rub you the wrong way. They may be parents, peers, or people you encounter in public. These people may not be likable; they may be generally unhappy people; they may have a chip on their shoulder or just a bad attitude towards others. No matter the reason, stay above the fray and maintain your respect for everyone.

R-E-S-P-E-C-T

– Aretha Franklin

Be Proud to Be a Teacher

MY DAD ONCE told me, "Being a teacher, you'll never be rich, but you'll never be poor either." First and foremost, we teachers are doing the job not because of the money, but because of the students in our classroom. They need our guidance, support, love, and commitment, as we prepare them as best we can to succeed in life. If we do the job right, we have a chance to inspire someone to achieve greatness. Pride in what you do will enhance the quality of everything you accomplish.

Come to think of it, Dad, I actually did become "rich" as a teacher . . . .

I'm never going to be a movie star.
But then, in all probability, Liz Taylor is never
going to teach first and second grade.

– *Mary J. Wilson*

If you can read this, thank a teacher.

– *Anonymous*

About the Author

VICKI HATHAWAY has been a public school teacher for more than thirty years. Throughout her career she has taught kindergarten, first, second, fourth, and sixth grades and today is a language arts consultant for all K–6 grades in the public school system in Enfield, Connecticut. She is also an adjunct professor at Saint Joseph College in West Hartford, Connecticut, teaching best practices in literacy education to elementary education graduate students. Vicki has three children and lives with her husband, George Hathaway, in Connecticut.